ART TREASURES OF ASIA

GENERAL EDITOR: JANE GASTON MAHLER

THE ART OF THE CHINESE SCULPTOR

Edited, with Introduction and Notes, by

Hugo Munsterberg

CHARLES E. TUTTLE COMPANY

RUTLAND, VERMONT & TOKYO, JAPAN

Contents

First edition, 1960. All rights reserved
Library of Congress Catalog Card No. 60-7251
Text printed by the Kenkyusha Printing Co., Tokyo. Color plates engraved and
printed by the Mitsumura Color Printing Co., Tokyo. Manufactured in Japan

Introduction

by Hugo Munsterberg

WHILE our grandparents thought of sculpture in terms of the marbles of the ancient Greeks, the carvings of the Gothic cathedrals, and the masterpieces of the great Renaissance sculptors, the 20th century, becoming aware of the beauty both of exotic and primitive civilizations, has broadened its outlook to include such diverse traditions as those of India and China, Negro Africa and Pre-Columbian America. Abandoning the classical premise that all great art was concerned with the beauty of the human body, we have discovered whole new worlds of aesthetic sensibility and enjoyment.

Among these, Chinese sculpture is one of the most remarkable and varied. Although the Chinese themselves have always regarded sculpture along with architecture as a mere craft rather than a major art form like painting and calligraphy, even they, influenced by Western appreciation of sculpture, have come to cherish it as one of the great manifestations of their artistic genius. The history of sculpture in China is a long and distinguished one, extending over a period of three thousand years from about the end of the second millenium before Christ through the 18th century, a history far older than that of European sculpture and covering a longer span of years even than that of the Egyptians.

Because of its long history, Chinese sculpture shows a great variety of styles, including some which are abstract and symbolical as well as others which are quite realistic. The choice of subject matter is also extremely varied. It may be derived from such diverse sources as the traditional Chinese nature deities, the gods and saints of Buddhism, the immortals of the Taoist legends, the sages and teachers of Confucianism, and, especially during the last centuries, the daily life of the Chinese people. The appeal of the sculpture is not confined to its artistic interest, for these carvings, which are a storehouse of traditional Chinese religion and folklore, serve as an ideal introduction to Chinese civilization.

The plastic arts of China are also remarkable for their diversity of media and techniques. Most common are such traditional materials as wood, bronze, glazed and unglazed clay, and various kinds of stone ranging from hard, highly polished marble to soft sandstone. At the same time the Chinese artist employs such peculiarly Chinese media as jade, which the Chinese love above all other stones, ivory, lacquer, bone, coral, soapstone, rock crystal, quartz, enamel, and porcelain. Although reproductions tend to reduce all these works to the same scale, they vary greatly in size, ranging from the monumental rock-cut sculptures of the cave temples to exquisite little carvings intended as jewels or ornaments. All of these different types have found enthusiastic collectors in China as well as in the West, and it is not uncommon to find connoisseurs who interest themselves in one particular medium, such as jade or ivory, almost to the exclusion of any other aspect of Chinese art.

The beginnings of Chinese sculpture go back to the earliest historical Chinese dynasty, known as the Shang, or Yin, which ruled from about 1550 to 1050 B.C. The most outstanding art works of the Shang period were the magnificent ceremonial bronzes ornamented with symbolical designs. These vessels, which no doubt had some primitive magical purpose, were sometimes made in the shape of animals such as the tiger, the water buffalo, the owl, and the pheasant. Their exact meaning is no longer known, but they probably represented the forces of nature which were worshipped by the Shang people. Their shapes are always strong and solid, perfectly balanced, yet dynamic with a wonderful feeling for the design as a whole and a perfect handling of the medium which reflected a highly developed bronze culture. At the Shang capital of Anyang, modern archeologists have also unearthed some stone sculptures representing various animals such as tigers, elephants, and owls, works which are of a cruder and less finished appearance than the bronzes, suggesting that stone sculpture was still in its beginnings, although these, too, show an instinctive sense of design and plastic form.

The Shang rulers were overthrown by the Chou dynasty which ruled China from about 1050 to

250 B.C., a period which saw the emergence of the Chinese nation as we know it today. In their art, the Chou people continued to produce much the same type of thing as the Shang Chinese had, with the bronze ceremonial vessels still predominant since they were so important in the rites performed for the ancestors and the deities. Many of these bronzes were also made in the form of animals which became less abstract, especially in the works from the end of the Chou rule. The most remarkable of these are the various dragons whose long curving bodies lent themselves to the more dramatic style popular in the later part of the period. During the last centuries of the Chou dynasty, sculpture in its own right began to emerge. Among the most popular were statues of human beings and horses which, in their greater naturalism both of subject and treatment, reflected a more humanistic spirit. Many subjects were represented, including imaginary spirits and symbolical beasts at one extreme, and at the other, realistic human figures such as servants or wrestlers. Most of the carvings which have come down to us are small in size, but literary accounts and recent archeological finds in South China would suggest that large-scale sculptures were also made, so that it is safe to say that by late Chou (600 B.C.), sculpture had emerged as a major art form.

The most glorious epoch in this early phase of Chinese civilization was the Han period, from about 200 B.C. to A.D. 200, during which a great empire extending from Central Asia in the west to Indo-China in the south was established. In the arts, sculpture showed a remarkable development which led to the emergence of monumental stone sculptures such as the horses and lions marking the tombs of the nobles. Although these large stone carvings are still somewhat crude, their primitive strength and simple, cubically conceived forms make them very impressive. Far more finished as well as more sophisticated are the horses of clay and jade found in the tombs of the period. Here the noble beauty of the horse is represented in a classical form which only the Greeks of the 6th and 5th centuries have rivalled, a form which combines vivid observation with a wonderful sculptural realization. Bronze vessels were less prominent since the outlook of the age was more secular than religious, but bronze continued to be used in vessels as well as sculptures, the most remarkable of which are a series of lovely dragons showing a graceful linear design, and charming little bears rendered in a very compact plastic manner. From an iconographic point of view,

the most interesting of the Han sculptures are the numerous slabs with relief carvings showing worldly scenes as well as scenes from the realm of the spirits. The emphasis is upon the dynamic treatment of line and the decorative pattern, both of which are characteristic of the Han artist.

The disintegration of the Han empire was followed by almost four centuries of strife which are called the period of the Six Dynasties after the six native ruling houses which continued to reign in South China while the whole of the northern part of the country was under the rule of the Wei Tartars. This period, which lasted until around A.D. 600, was one of great artistic growth in spite of the political, military, and economic difficulties which the country experienced. The six southern dynasties, especially the Liang which ruled during the 6th century, were all patrons of the traditional arts, and the large stone lions and chimera flanking the approaches to the graves of the Liang emperor Wu Ti are among the masterpieces of Chinese sculpture. They are at once bolder and more dynamic than the large Han figures, with a forceful sweep of line and an expressive vitality which give them a true grandeur. The numerous clay tomb figurines show that this art continued to flourish. A great variety were produced, including many animals, such as horses, camels, and dragons, human figures of all types, and various buildings which give an insight into the architecture of the period.

Far more important for the history of Chinese sculpture were the developments which were taking place in Northern China where the foreign rulers had established a variety of new dynasties, the most important of which is the Wei. Although originally "western barbarians" from Central Asia, these new rulers adopted Chinese customs and were soon absorbed into the culture, becoming fervent Buddhists and thus of great importance in the development of Chinese Buddhist art.

Buddhism, an Indian religion founded by Gautama Buddha during the 6th century before Christ had begun to reach China during the last years of the Han rule, but it was not until the Six Dynasties period that it became really popular. By the 6th century, it had been so widely accepted that one could speak of China as a predominantly Buddhist country although Confucianism and Taoism continued to flourish. The essential doctrine taught by the Buddha is that in life there is suffering, that this suffering springs from desire, and that only through renunciation can we be delivered and enter Nirvana ie ultimate nothingness or, as later Buddhism taught, the Buddhist paradise. The Buddha himself had been born a royal prince, but after an encounter with an old man, a cripple, a corpse, and an ascetic he renounced his heritage and his princely garments to become an ascetic. However, this life did not bring him fulfillment and one day while meditating under the Tree of Wisdom, he experienced what in Buddhist terminology is called Enlightenment. In an instant, everything became clear — the nature of life, the root of suffering, the Nirvana, and at that moment he became the Enlightened One, or the Buddha. Then, dressed in the robe of a monk, he traveled all over India collecting alms and preaching the gospel of compassion.

The figure of this great teacher gave rise to one of the most moving religious symbols ever created, namely the Buddha image. No other religious leader has been represented in so universally meaningful a way, and millions of people who know nothing about Buddhist doctrine are familiar with these figures of the Buddha which are found all over Southern and Eastern Asia. The earlier and simpler type of Buddhism was concerned with the Buddha as a sage, but as Buddhism developed, the historical Buddha was transformed into a god who was only one of many such Buddhas that had preceded him or were to come. Among the most important of these other Buddhas represented in Chinese sculpture are the Buddhas of the Past, often seen on Buddhist steles; the Buddha of the Future, or Maitreya; the Buddha of Endless Light, or Amitabha, who rules in the Western Paradise; the Cosmic Buddha, Vairocana, of whom all Buddhas and all beings are but emanations; and the Buddha of Medicine and Healing, or Bhaishajyaguru. In addition to the various Buddhas, there are also many Buddhist saints, or Bodhisattvas; holy men, or Arhats; and numroues lesser sacred figures, such as angels and guardians.

Of all the thousands of images of the Buddhist pantheon which were made during the Six Dynasties period, the most impressive are the sculptures of the rock-cut cave temples of Northern China, notably those at Yün-kang and Lung-men. Under imperial patronage, dozens of caves were hollowed out of hillsides, a custom which was undoubtedly derived from India where, from earliest times, temples had been carved out of rock. The walls and ceilings of these cave shrines were covered with thousands of figures of Buddhas, Bodhisattvas, Arhats, angels, and all kinds of animal and vegetable motifs of a symbolical or ornamental character. We are told that in the year A.D. 523, 800,000 labor days were expended at Lung-men alone, which was but one of the numerous cave sites. Individual figures like that of the Giant Buddha at Yün-kang were as much as fifty feet high, a testimony not only to the skill of the carvers but to the great role which Buddhism played in the life of the people.

The style of these statues is based on Indian works, especially the so-called Greco-Buddhist prototypes from Gandhara in northwestern India. Gradually, however, the style was modified by Chinese ideals. The rather sensuous and full forms of India became flatter and more linear, resembling those of early Medieval European art, as is best seen in the Wei images of the 6th century. Here, in this abstract, deeply spiritual style, the Buddhist faith finds its most profound expression.

Besides these cave sculptures, there were also individual statues of Buddha and the Buddhist saints. Among these, the most beautiful as well as the most common are the images made of gilt bronze. They exist in great numbers even today, most of them small in size though no doubt many bigger ones were made and then melted down for their metal by later unbelieving ages. Since quite a few of the statues are dated, they are particularly interesting from a historical point of view, enabling us to reconstruct the development of Chinese Buddhist sculpture.

The early style of the 4th century and the first part of the 5th century is based on Gandharan and Central Asian models, while the later, more abstract style of the end of the 5th and the first half of the 6th century is more characteristically Chinese. Both styles are well represented in these Buddhist bronzes, many of which show the superb mastery of the sculptors. Although the artists were anonymous craftsmen, one would have to turn to ancient Greece or southern India to find bronzes of equal skill and expressiveness.

Other characteristically Chinese types of sculpture were the stone steles which usually represent Buddhist scenes in relief, with the Buddha in the center surrounded by monks, Bodhisattvas, guardians, lions, and angels. Often an incense burner and worshippers are portrayed beneath the sacred figures. Other scenes show Maitreya, the Buddha of the Future, as a Bodhisattva seated in meditation in the Tusita heaven; or the historical Buddha in conversation with Prabhutaratna, the Buddha of the Past who preceded him. Another common scene is that of Buddha as a royal prince seated beneath the Tree of Enlightenment. A favorite symbol is the lotus flower which occurs in all Buddhist art and represents purity, for just as the lotus emerges pure from the mud at the bottom of the pond, so the Buddha traveled through the world but was unstained by its corruption. The style in these steles is typically Chinese with its emphasis upon a linear pattern and its reduction of all forms to a flat abstract design. As in the contemporary bronzes and stone sculpture, the human figures are elongated and the drapery is reduced to cascades of curving lines with wing-like edges. Chinese iconographical elements, such as the dragon, are sometimes introduced, but by and large the Northern Wei sculptures combine a strictly Indian iconography with a characteristically Chinese style.

After centuries of disunity, China was united by the rulers of the Sui dynasty which lasted from 581 to 618, a reign brief in years but of great importance politically as well as artistically. Buddhist sculpture flourished, and a new style emerged, showing a revival of Indian influence in its greater naturalism and its more plastic cylindrical forms.

Among the many outstanding examples of Sui sculpture, the finest are the free standing figures of Buddhas and Bodhisattvas which show a wonderful sense of the three dimensional form. The very essence of the body is brought out by emphasizing the simple, geometric shape, and articulating the surface by the folds of the garment. Cave temples continued to be carved, the most important of which are at Lung-men and T'ien-lung Shan; and bronze sculptures were made which are often of great charm and beauty.

With the establishment of the T'ang dynasty in 618, China entered what many people have regarded as its most glorious period. Once again unified and powerful, the country expanded far into Central Asia, and foreign merchants and travelers were a common sight in the streets of the capital city of Ch'ang-an. Buddhist monks crossed the deserts of Central Asia to visit the holy cities of Buddhism in India from which they brought back not only sacred writings but images and paintings as well. The most famous of these monks was Hsüan-tsang whose record of his trip is still a valuable source of information. Interestingly enough, he reported that Buddhism, which was then flourishing in China and Central Asia, had lost its appeal in India, where many of the holy places were being neglected.

Unfortunately, only a fraction of T'ang art ha survived, but from literary records and existin T'ang works, we get some idea of the magnificenc of this civilization. It was not only the age o China's two most famous poets, Li Po and Tu Fu and immortal painters like Wang Wei and W Tao-tzu, it was also a period of brilliant develop ment in the decorative arts, such as ceramics, lac quer, metal ware, textiles, glass, and the like. It ha been justly said that the Chinese civilization of tha time was the most remarkable in the world.

T'ang sculpture also flourished, the religious a well as the secular. The most marked change wa a greater emphasis upon the beauty of the huma body, which was shown with full, rounded forms an swaying curves. So pronounced was this new de velopment (which was brought about by the re newed contacts with India as well as a tendenc towards greater naturalism) that contemporary crit ics complained of the fact that the Bodhisattva looked like dancing girls. The result is an art which especially in the early part of the T'ang period, o the 7th century, has a warm and sensuous appeal although it has lost some of the spiritual qualit which made the 6th century images so moving During the later T'ang period, when a more esoteri type of Buddhism became popular, a dry and les convincing style prevailed, but relatively few ex amples of this have been preserved.

The most important cave sites continued to b Lung-men and T'ien-lung Shan in Honan an Shansi provinces respectively. Of the Lung-me statues of this period, the most impressive is a gian image over eighty feet high of the Cosmic Buddha Vairocana, who, among contemporary sects, en joyed great popularity. The T'ien-lung Shan cave are noted for their strong Indian influence which i reflected in carvings of a voluptuous quality quit alien to the more characteristically Chinese tradi tion. At these sites and others, literally thousands o Buddhist images were carved out of rock, almost al of them of remarkably high quality.

In addition to the stone sculptures all the othe media, such as wood, clay, metal, and ivory, con tinued to be used. Bronze was apparently somewha less important than it had been previously, althoug this may well be an erroneous impression caused b the fact that in later periods the larger bronzes wer melted down. In any case, the smaller ones which do survive indicate that an excellent level of crafts manship continued to be maintained. A new em phasis was placed on lacquer sculpture either with a wooden core or hollow. The latter method, an especially important discovery, played a significant role in both Chinese and Japanese sculpture. A wooden skeleton was covered with cloth soaked in lacquer which was then usually gilded. The resulting statues were so light that they could easily be carried around in processions or taken out of the temples in case of fire. Relatively few of these images have been preserved but there can be no doubt that they were once plentiful, as they were in Japan where many examples have survived.

Of all T'ang sculptures, the best known are the tomb figurines of which countless numbers have been preserved. No collection of Chinese art in any Western museum is complete without its grave figures, and thousands of private collections can boast of at least a few. Made of plain or glazed clay and often manufactured in huge quantities with the help of molds, they are readily available today and are so popular that they have been forged on a vast scale. Although they were produced by simple artisans, the quality was often so fine that they compare favorably with the best of the stone sculptures.

Of the various subjects found among the grave figures, the most beautiful, perhaps, are the horses, various types of which were portrayed, such as cavalry chargers or mounts of ladies and gentlemen of the court. Some have saddles, others are bare back, and they are shown standing still, or pawing, or galloping, different poses which reveal a complete mastery of the form. They are modelled with simplicity, the details subordinate to the beauty of the shape itself, and the result is works which rank among the finest of equestrian statues. All these horses stand on a rectangular base, and are hollow inside with an opening in the belly. Some are glazed, the colors usually being brown, straw, or amber with splashes of blue or green added to the saddle, harness, or similar details. Others are unglazed with a little unfired pigment added, usually red. Besides the horses, there are camels which were so important in the long trips across the deserts of Central Asia; bullocks pulling carts; dogs and other domestic animals; birds; and imaginary and fantastic creatures, half animal and half human. In addition to the various animals, there are all sorts of human figures, among the most delightful of which are those of T'ang beauties with their full faces, high painted eyebrows, narrow eyes, and elaborate hairdos, and various dancers and musicians which give us a charming glimpse into the T'ang world. Many foreigners, such as merchants, grooms, and cara-

vaneers add a colorful note. Buddhist sculpture is not found in the tombs except for the guardian figures who are represented as Chinese warriors dressed in elaborate armor.

The disintegration of the T'ang empire was accompanied by the chaos of civil war. This period, extending from 908 to 960, is called the Five Dynasties period, a time of disunity which was followed by the Sung dynasty, which lasted from 960 to 1279. During these three centuries, Buddhism steadily declined, and only the Ch'an sect, better known by the Japanese name Zen, continued to flourish as well as to exert great influence on the culture. Since Ch'an Buddhism required no images of deities, using instead the portraits of its patriarchs, painting became the dominant art. Chinese sculpture never again recovered its pre-eminence, nor did it regain the vitality which it had shown in previous centuries. It would seem that the Buddhist church had been a necessary source both of inspiration and patronage, and that as Buddhism lost its hold, the great tradition of sculpture also fell into a decline.

In keeping with the spirit of the age, the deities represented were less austere, and the most popular Buddhist figure became that of Kuan Yin, the Bodhisattva of Mercy, who was often shown as a female deity to emphasize the attributes of gentleness and compassion. The large-scale figures are usually seated in the position of royal ease, relaxed, even languid, with one leg pendant. The forms are softer and more natural, and polychromed wood was preferred to stone, for it lent itself better to the fluid, painterly effects which the sculptors wished to achieve. Their bright colors, along with their sophistication and virtuosity of technique, made them justly popular with collectors.

Stone sculpture suffered a marked decline, for it was less well suited to the kind of sculpture in vogue. Cave temples were no longer carved at the great sites of the T'ang period, such as Lung-men and T'ien-lung Shan, but a few were still made at more provincial sites in Kansu and Szechuan. Bronze sculpture also suffered, but there are some graceful bronze images of Sung date which show that this art form still maintained its high level of craftsmanship. Among the clay sculptures, the most outstanding are a group of Arhats, or Lohans as the Chinese call them, which originally came from a monastery at I-chou near Peking, but which today are divided among several museums, the majority in the United States. They are monumental in scale, the seated figures some $3\frac{1}{2}$ feet high, glazed in three

(continued on page 32)

Water Buffalo Bronze Vessel

Ca. 1100 B.C. Shang period
6 ¹/₂" high, 8 ¹/₂" long
Courtesy of the Fogg Museum, Cambridge, Massachusetts

VESSELS like this bronze water buffalo were made by the ancient Chinese of the Shang and Chou periods for offering sacrifices to the spirits of the ancestors and the forces of nature, such as wind or rain. Although this particular work looks like a piece of sculpture, it is actually a wine vessel from which libations were offered. The head and the back of the animal form a kind of cover with the horns and the small dragon making up the handle. The technique used in casting these vessels is called *cire perdue*, or the lost-wax method, in which a solid core of some material like clay was painted with thin layers of wax until a coating of the required thickness was attained. The design was carved into the wax, and the whole was covered with a mold of clay containing vents to let the melted wax run out when the hot liquid bronze was poured into the mold. Originally, these vessels had a silvery tone, but over the centuries a patina has formed, often green, which has greatly enhanced the color. This water buffalo, which was made about a thousand years before Christ, has a simple, plastic form with only the most essential detail. The smooth, softly rounded undecorated body is set off against the curves of the dragon and the simple linear pattern on the horns and the face. Since the water buffalo has crescent shaped horns which resemble the half moon, and since the moon in ancient Chinese folk lore is connected with rain and water, it has been suggested that the animal is a lunar and rain symbol, but at this point of our knowledge, such a conclusion cannot be stated with certainty. There is no doubt, however, that this beautiful bronze was not just a work of art but had a symbolical meaning as well.

PLATE TWO

Jade Finial in Human and Animal Form

Ca. 900 B.C. Chou period
2 ¹/₃" high, 2 ⁴/₅" wide
Courtesy of the Fogg Museum, Cambridge, Massachusetts

THROUGHOUT Chinese history, jade has been considered a particularly precious stone, and Chinese craftsmen have used it for carvings and jewels of all types. This particular jade, which probably dates from around 900 B.C., is very interesting not only for its artistic excellence but also for its strange iconography. Although the exact symbolism of these ancient jade ornaments is no longer known, there can be little doubt that they were not simply decorative but had some deeper meaning, as does this jade carving from the Chou period. It is a finial consisting of a human head with Mongoloid features and ears with large holes; beneath the head, a small rectangular object with a round indentation; two birds projecting out at the sides; and at the bottom, the head of a horned animal which appears to be a ram. Since the bird in Chinese art is a symbol both of the South and the sun and the ancient pictograph for sun is very similar to the emblem appearing on the image, it would appear that the man-like figure is a sky deity, in which case the horned animal would be a lunar symbol so that the whole would represent the sky god of ancient China who presides over the sun and the moon and rules heaven. This type of symbolism is quite common during Shang and Chou times, and is often found on the bronzes and jades of the period. In keeping with the symbolical ideas, the various elements of this jade are represented in an abstract manner, yet at the same time, the emphasis on the design and the skill of the carving give it a remarkable formal beauty.

PLATE THREE

Gilt Bronze Dragon

Ca. A.D. 200. Han period
2 3/5″ high, 4 4/5″ long
Courtesy of the Fogg Museum, Cambridge, Massachusetts

THE DRAGON in Western mythology represents the forces of evil which are overcome by such culture heroes as Siegfried in the tale of the Niebelungen and St. George in the Christian legend, but in China the dragon is an auspicious and benevolent creature. He is connected with the sky, rain, clouds, mist, and the mysterious ultimate essence which the Chinese call the Tao. He is also a symbol of the ancestors, and he is associated with the imperial power, for the emperor, or the Son of Heaven, ruled on the dragon throne in Peking, and the robes of high government officials were decorated with dragons. In popular culture, the dragon festival and the dragon boat were very prominent, for the dragon is one of the most beloved symbols in Chinese art, appearing again and again in all media from the very earliest of Shang objects to works of the present day. Since the slender, undulating form of the dragon is so perfectly suited to the calligraphic tradition of Chinese art, this mysterious animal has always been a favorite subject. In Han art, the dragon is often used as a symbol of the East, appearing with the tiger, the bird, and the tortoise in combat with the snake which represent the four directions. This graceful and elegant gilt bronze is one of the loveliest of Chinese dragons and it is typical of the Han period in its abstract and simple style. The figure is reduced to a dynamic linear pattern with a strong sense of movement in the swinging curves emphasized at the expense of plastic form, and creating a very expressive piece of sculpture.

Stone Figure of Seated Bodhisattva

From Lung-men, ca. A.D. 500. Six Dynasties period
17 ¹/₂" high, 9 ¹/₂" wide
Courtesy of Mr. and Mrs. J. W. Alsdorf, Winnetka, Illinois

THIS BEAUTIFUL stone carving is one of the thousands of works which once filled the famous Buddhist caves at Lung-men in North China, a testimony to the religious fervor of the age, for these figures were dedicated by the devout as acts of merit. Judging from the headdress and the princely garment, this figure is a Bodhisattva, one of the Buddhist saints. The position of the legs suggests that it is a representation of Maitreya, the Buddha of the Future, seen here in his incarnation as a Bodhisattva awaiting Buddhahood. One of his hands is lifted in the *abhaya mudra,* the gesture of fearlessness, while the other is lowered in the *vara mudra,* the gesture of charity. The face is profoundly spiritual, the eyes lowered instead of looking out, symbolizing the deep meditation of the deity. The abstract style is typical of the works of the very early 6th century. The human figure is flattened and distorted as it was in Romanesque sculpture, a device used to bring out the otherworldly nature of the deity. Although based on Indian and Central Asian prototypes, the statue is wholly Chinese in style. The reduction of the body and drapery to a two-dimensional geometric design with strong linear accents is characteristic of the native tradition in contrast to the fuller and more sensual sculpture which prevailed in India. Although made by an unknown craftsman, this carving belongs among the masterpieces of religious sculpture.

Gilded Bronze Figure of Arhat

Ca. A.D. 500. Six Dynasties period
5 3/5" high
Courtesy of the Fogg Museum, Cambridge, Massachusetts

CHINESE Buddhist bronzes, especially those of the 6th and 7th centuries, are outstanding both from a purely artistic point of view and for the depth of their spiritual feeling. In them the whole of the Buddhist pantheon is represented from the loftiest deities to the humblest of human and animal figures. Especially fine are the numerous representations of the various Buddhas and Bodhisattvas in whom the Buddhist ideals of inner peace find perfect expression. This image shows yet another Buddhist conception, namely that of an Arhat, or Lohan in Chinese, one of the holy men who had devoted their lives to meditation and good deeds. Originally there were sixteen of them who were instructed by the Buddha Sakyamuni to remain in the world and follow him; later, this number was expanded until these holy men were sometimes represented in a group of five hundred. They are always shown as monks dressed in monks' robes; their heads are shaven and lack the *ushnisha*, or protuberance symbolizing the supermind, which is the mark of a Buddha. This particular Arhat, however, has an *urna*, or third eye, on his forehead, which is a symbol of supernatural vision. Particularly fine is the deeply moving face in which the spiritual dedication of the holy figure is expressed. The body is treated in an abstract manner, only the head and the hands standing out against the exaggerated drapery, which is arranged in a series of projecting, leaf-like folds that are typical for the style of the early 6th century. Such Buddhist bronzes, of which this is a fine example, represent one of the high points in the Buddhist art of China.

Stone Carving of Kuan Yin

Ca. A.D. 600. Sui period
40" high
Courtesy of Mr. Earl Morse, New York

OUTSTANDING among Buddhist images is this Avalokitesvara, or Kuan Yin, the Bodhisattva of Mercy and Compassion, a typical work of the Sui period, that is, the last years of the 6th and the beginning of the 7th century. Carved in stone by anonymous craftsmen, it is a free standing sculpture rather than a wall carving from a cave. Originally the statue was painted at least in part, and traces of color are still visible, most noticeably the red which decorates the girdle and many of the ornaments. Since the image is of a Bodhisattva rather than a Buddha, the garments are those of an Indian prince with various scarves and jewels. The right arm is broken off at the elbow, but the hand was probably raised in the *abhaya mudra*, the gesture meaning that the faithful should have no fear but should put their trust in Avalokitesvara. The left hand holds a bottle of heavenly nectar, a sign of immortality. The head, erect and frontal, shows the calm serenity of one who, having overcome the suffering of this world, has found peace in the lotus of the good law. The form is wonderfully plastic with a strong emphasis upon the cylindrical shape of the body, which is typical for Sui sculpture. The verticals of the body are varied by the rich pattern of the jewels and drapery which curve and cross and intersect, and by the details of the ornaments, especially in the headdress and the skirt. The back view of the figure is particularly lovely, with its abstract design of the human body and the drapery. Such a sculpture should, of course, be experienced as a work in the round, for it is the three-dimensional quality of the carvings which gives them their unique appeal.

PLATE SEVEN

Stone Lion

Ca. A.D. 700. T'ang period
9" high, 5" wide
Courtesy of Mr. and Mrs. J. W. Alsdorf, Winnetka, Illinois

THE LION, although quite common in Chinese art, is actually not native to China where the tiger was the symbol of strength and valor. It was introduced, as were so many other motifs, from Central Asia and ultimately from the Near East where the lion is often found in Assyrian and Babylonian art. In China, it was regarded as a royal symbol, designating power and kingly rule, and lions were often seen flanking the Buddha's throne as a sign that the Buddha is the lion among men and the ruler of the universe. This statue was probably one of a pair used in some such fashion. The mouth is snarling, opening as if in a roar to scare away any demons which might wish to harm the Buddha. The head is vigorously rendered, and there is a strong plastic feeling in the body with its broad chest and heavy, massive legs which rest upon exaggerated claws. Although the artist has observed nature, he is interested not in a literal realism of the kind often found in the animal sculptures of the 19th century, but in a more general expression of the strength and beauty of the lion. The result is a modified naturalism typical of the T'ang period. The vitality of this work would suggest that it was carved during the most creative years of the T'ang dynasty, namely the 7th century which many critics regard as the Golden Age of Chinese art.

PLATE EIGHT

Unglazed Clay Horse

Ca. A.D. 700. T'ang period
20 3/4" high, 23 3/4" long
Courtesy of Mr. and Mrs. J. W. Alsdorf, Winnetka Illinois

AMONG the numerous figures found in the ancient Chinese graves, the most beautiful are
the horses. The earliest of these date from the late Chou period; they became popular during
Han times when the Chinese had many contacts with the people of the steppes, and they
were very common during the Six Dynasties and T'ang periods. This example, which is
exquisitely modelled, is unglazed, with brownish earth clinging to the light-colored body
and traces of red on the saddle. The horse is represented in a very life-like way, showing
the naturalism of the T'ang period, yet no detail is allowed to obscure the essential form
of the horse which is brought out in all its beauty. The rounded shape of the body is finely
balanced on the tensed legs, one of which is raised as if the animal were pawing; the neck
is arched, with the head slightly turned; and the curve of the tail repeats in reverse the curve
of the rump. The smooth surface of the body is contrasted with the linear design of the
mane, the folds of the saddle cloth, and the muscles in the legs and face. Particularly fine
is the spirited expression of the head, with the pricked up ears and open mouth. The figure
is at once strong and graceful, perfectly balanced and expressive, yet it is not a solitary
masterpiece by some Chinese Rodin but the production of an ordinary artisan who no
doubt made thousands of tomb figures for his living.

Three-Color Pottery Figure

Ca. A.D. 700. T'ang period
13 ¹/₂" high, 4 ¹/₂" wide
Courtesy of Mr. and Mrs. J. W. Alsdorf, Winnetka, Illinois

THIS CHARMING figure of a T'ang lady is one of the many thousands of such statuettes found in the tombs of the period. Originally probably a substitute for human sacrifice, these tomb figures became very popular in Han times and reached their climax during the T'ang period. Often the statues of entire noble families with their servants and animals were placed in the tombs, the idea being that they would accompany the honored dead into the after world. Typical of the 8th century ideal of feminine beauty, this figure is shown with the moon face so much admired at the time, a small mouth, narrow eyes, full cheeks, and pale skin contrasted with dark hair. Both the facial expression and the pose indicate the modest demeanor of a lady. She is dressed in a simple gown covered with a blue, yellow, and green glaze which is often found in T'ang ceramics and is known as three-color ware. The hands are hidden by the folds of the shawl, and a long narrow skirt reveals only the up-turned tips of the shoes. The forms are extremely simple, with the slender body balanced against the full round shape of the head. Although the style is a naturalistic one, it is both simplified and general, for this is not the portrait of one particular woman but rather of a certain type of person. In spite of the fact that these figures were intended for tombs, to be buried and not to be enjoyed by the public, many of them were real works of art, combining a fresh charm with a beauty of modelling and glaze.

PLATE TEN

Polychrome Wooden Bodhisattva

Ca. 1000. Sung period
46" high
Courtesy of Miss Alice Boney, New York

WHILE stone and bronze were the most popular media of the T'ang period, the Sung sculptors preferred wood, which was better suited to the soft painterly style in vogue during this age of refinement and sophistication. This example, which represents a seated Bodhisattva, is particularly fine not only for its sculptural quality but also because of the excellently preserved colors. Mellowed by age, they give a soft beauty to the figure, with subtle reds and blues in the garment, white in the borders, and white and gold in the ornaments. Even such a minute detail as the thin pencil line of the mustache, an indication that this is an Indian deity, is clearly preserved. Although the exact identity of this Bodhisattva is not indicated, it is probably a representation of Kuan Yin, the Compassionate One, the Ocean of Pity, who was especially popular during the Sung period. Kuan Yin appears in no less than 108 manifestations, some of them female. He is shown in the Yogi position, or the pose of meditation in which the legs are crossed and the soles of the feet turned up. His right hand is in the *vara mudra*, the gesture of charity, while his left hand seems to suggest the *mudra* of argumentation. Originally, his forehead had some kind of jewel for the *urna*, or third eye, indicating that he sees all and that no suffering escapes the Lord of Compassion who had delayed his own entrance into paradise in order to bring salvation to man. The forms of the sculpture are strong and plastic, combining a graceful physical beauty with a spiritual strength.

Ivory Figure of Kuan Yin with Child

Ca. 1500. Ming period
7" high
Courtesy of Mr. and Mrs. Francis Reif, Vancouver, British Columbia

THIS EXQUISITE piece is one of the many remarkable carvings in the Reif collection of Chinese ivories. Representing Kuan Yin in female form with a child, it is particularly interesting for its iconography. Although originally a male deity like all the other Buddhist figures, Kuan Yin, beginning with the Sung period, was often shown as a female due to the fact that the Bodhisattva had become identified with a local Chinese mother goddess, "bringer of children," and also because the gentleness and compassion of the deity suggest feminine qualities. The representation of Kuan Yin as a kind of Madonna at once recalls the Christian art of the West, but it seems unlikely that the Chinese were familiar with European art as early as the 12th century when these images began to appear. The tender, smiling expression of Kuan Yin's plump face and the natural way she holds the child, clasped loosely, and nestled against the body, gives the figure a feeling of maternal warmth. The quality of the carving is excellent, showing a delicacy combined with strength. The form is solid and full, and the lines of the drapery make a pattern of curves which repeat and contrast with one another in rhythmic succession. In spite of the small scale, these ivory carvings often possess a kind of monumentality, revealing a better understanding of the nature of sculpture than do the larger images of the period.

White Porcelain Pu-tai

Ca. 1700. Ch'ing period
6 1/2" high, 6" wide
Courtesy of Mr. Warren Cox, New York

THE WHITE porcelain figures made in Fukien province and better known in the West as Blanc-de-Chine ware have enjoyed great popularity among modern collectors. At a period when Chinese sculpture as a whole had suffered decline if not total eclipse, they preserved much of the great plastic tradition so characteristic of Chinese art. Originating during the last years of the Ming dynasty, the earliest of these figures date from the first part of the 17th century. However, most of them come from the Ch'ing period, and although they continued to be made through the 19th and into the 20th century, the quality of the later works deteriorated. Among the deities represented, the most interesting are Kuan Yin, shown as an elegant lady, and Pu-tai, or Hotei as he is called in Japanese. This delightful figure is one of the seven gods of good luck, and he is always shown with a laughing face and a bulging belly to indicate his happiness. It is believed that the prototype of the god was a 10th century Taoist monk who in later times was looked upon as a manifestation of Mi-lo, or Maitreya, the Buddha of the Future. Here, the emphasis is upon the compact roundness of the figure, with the large belly as the center, and legs and arms drawn close, so that the whole is confined to a rough circle. The porcelain is very pure and the white glaze is clear, indicating the perfect technique which the Ch'ing potters had evolved. Although lacking the power and intensity of earlier Chinese sculpture, these last works are full of life and charm.

(continued from page 7)

colors, and realistic in execution. Each face expresses serenity or intense thought. On the whole, however, clay sculpture showed the same loss of vitality which affected the other media.

The Yüan dynasty, established by the Mongol invaders and lasting from 1280 to 1368, brought little new to sculpture, which for the most part continued in the late Sung style. During the Ming period, under a native dynasty that ruled for almost three centuries until 1644, religious sculpture kept up the earlier iconographic traditions, but showed a loss both of artistic vitality and religious intensity. Some of the statues continued to be made of stone and wood and bronze, but the Ming sculptors preferred to work in clay which had a wooden core and was covered with brilliant colors. The result is a naturalistic and often very garish art which has none of the depth of feeling or beauty of form found in the works of earlier centuries. Perhaps the most interesting of the Ming images are the groups of the Five Hundred Arhats who are seen seated in the dim interiors of temples as if they were real monks. Artistically they are quite undistinguished, of poor quality, and marked by a crude realism. Also interesting are the brightly colored figures of Taoist deities with their imaginative and fairy-tale-like appearance. To guard the spirit path to the mausoleums of the Ming rulers near Peking, monumental stone sculpture was still produced, although the camels, elephants, and chimeras have none of the vitality of earlier periods.

The most rewarding examples of Ming period work are not the large stone or clay pieces but rather those on a small scale, notably in ivory, porcelain, and jade, which have found many admirers among modern collectors. The deities shown are usually either of Buddhist derivation, like Kuan Yin or Pu Tai, or Taoist, such as Lao-tzu, the founder of the Taoist sect, and Shou Lao, the god of long life. Other popular figures are Kuan Ti, the god of war, and lucky deities, fairies, and auspicious personages. In keeping with their size, they have a fine sense of detail and an exquisite and often intricate technique.

The porcelain figures were either done in three-colored ware with bold, bright designs in red, yellow, and green or cobalt (later turquoise and buff), or in plain white. Artistically speaking, the latter are superior and under the name of Blanc de Chine (also called Fukien ware) were very popular with Western collectors. The numerous representations of Kuan Yin are especially graceful, with their flowing lines and their pure white body and glaze. Ivory, which had already been used by the T'ang and Sung carvers, became very popular, and the finest of the Ming ivories are particularly lovely with their rich yellowish color and their exquisite carving. Another favorite medium was jade in which the beauty of the material itself as well as the intricate detail of the workmanship was highly valued. For those who prefer sophistication and perfection of technique over primitive simplicity or expressive power, these works will be among the treasures of Chinese art.

In 1644 the Ming dynasty was overthrown by the foreign Manchu, nomad tribes who founded the Ch'ing dynasty which lasted until the establishment of the Chinese Republic in 1912. In sculpture it was a sterile period; no new development took place, and monumental sculpture in all media ceased to be of any significance, although porcelains, jades, and ivories continued to flourish at least through the 18th century. Neither subject nor style differed substantially from that of the Ming period, although there was even more emphasis upon intricate detail for the sake of virtuosity. The glaze of the Fukien wares tends to be thinner and more vitreous, and the expression of the figures less convincing, although individual pieces are still quite lovely. The colored figures, especially those of the K'ang Hsi period, are more decorative and elegant, but they lack some of the strength of the Ming wares. The jade carvings, especially of the 18th century, were sometimes incredibly elaborate. A favorite subject was the Hills of the Immortals carved in complicated detail with Taoist figures, storks (a symbol of long life), rocks, a pavilion, trees, and staircases. Although these jades have a certain charm, they are more curiosities than works of art, reflecting in their fussy ornateness a society which valued mere skill over true artistic qualities. After the Ch'ien Lung period (1736–95) the arts fell into a gradual decay, and by the end of the 19th century, the great artistic tradition of China had come to an end.